PIER 21

Listen to My Story

Christine Welldon

NIMBUS
PUBLISHING

This book is dedicated to my parents, who chose Canada.

Nimbus Publishing Limited
3731 Mackintosh St, Halifax, NS B3K 5A5
(902) 455-4286 nimbus.ca

Printed and bound in Canada

Pier 21 song excerpt reprinted with permission of Lennie Gallant, Wendy Gilmour

English John's story is adapted from the book *British Home Children* by D. Phyllis Harrison (1979) and appears courtesy of J. Gordon Shillingford Publishing.

Author photo: Photo Shop, Toronto
Interior design: Andrew Herygers
Cover design: Kate Westphal, Graphic Detail Inc.

Library and Archives Canada Cataloguing in Publication

    Welldon, Christine
    Listen to my story : Pier 21 / Christine Welldon.
    Includes bibliographical references.
    ISBN 978-1-55109-909-5

1. Ports of entry—Nova Scotia—Halifax—History—20th century—Juvenile literature.
2. Canada—Emigration and immigration—History—20th century—Juvenile literature.
3. Immigrants—Canada—History—20th century—Juvenile literature. I. Title.

JV7225.W42 2012   j325.71   C2011-907640-3

Nimbus Publishing acknowledges the financial support for its publishing activities from the Government of Canada through the Canada Book Fund (CBF) and the Canada Council for the Arts, and from the Province of Nova Scotia through the Department of Communities, Culture and Heritage.

I've seen them arrive here
All nervous and worn
Like they had found calm
In the eye of the storm,
Orphans and refugees
Seeking a home,
Healing for hearts that are torn.
— Lennie Gallant

"Will the moon come to Canada with us?"
— Immigrant child

Table of Contents

Introduction

The new sights and sounds after a long Atlantic crossing were an exciting but exhausting experience for young travellers like these.

Listen to my story: Pier 21

Here is a gateway. Through its doors pass an orphaned boy dressed in rags, escaping from a terrible war, a young girl with her shoes in tatters, a new bride with a baby in her arms, a hopeful family carrying all they have left in the world, a wounded soldier returning from battle. Imagine each of these and multiply them by many thousands. These are people who entered Canada through **Pier** 21, the gateway to freedom. It is a place of voices, all speaking at once, in many languages. Each voice has a story to tell, of loss and hope, of capture and escape, of defeat and victory. In fact, if you pay close attention, you can hear the voices echoing around these old walls.

"Here is my story," they call. "Pull up a chair. Listen!"

A very busy place!

When ships docked at Pier 21, immigrants[1] walked into a busy hive of activity on the second floor. There were customs officers and translators, Red Cross volunteers and nurses, a counter for money exchange, a doctor's office and hospital quarters, a cafeteria and kitchen. There was a nursery for the babies, a canteen for supplies, and sleeping quarters for those who needed to stay overnight. There was plenty of room for all of these services. At 2 storeys high and 183 metres long, Pier 21 covered an area of 6,700 square metres. The first floor was a storage area that held freight from ships, while the second floor was used to greet newcomers.

1. Check the Glossary on page 78 for definitions of all the words you see in blue!

A Day at Pier 21

Imagine you are at Pier 21 after a long Atlantic crossing to Halifax, Nova Scotia. You leave the ship and enter the large immigration hall on the second floor. You are with hundreds of people who want to enter Canada. They are sitting and waiting to be called, walking about, or standing in groups expressing their hopes and fears to one another in many languages.

You see people lining up to buy train tickets or exchange money, and the floors are littered with orange peels, cornflakes, and discarded papers. You hear mothers calling to their playful children and loudspeakers giving information. There is a smell of decaying food, brought from the home country, and the sharp smell of **prosciutto** and dried fish lying on a table with other **confiscated** foods.

No octopus allowed!

The assembly room at Pier 21 could hold only 250 people at a time. The seats were always full because as soon as one group of immigrants left, the next group was led in. One day, the guards noticed a few seats were empty around a man who sat holding a package on his lap. No one was sitting beside him, and the guards soon found out why. He was holding a package of dried octopus he had brought with him on his long journey. It was beginning to smell!

Posters tempted new Canadians to try their luck in the Canadian West. Many travelled onward from Pier 21 to Alberta or Saskatchewan by train, gazing out the window at the forested land and wide-open skies.

For almost fifty years, these were the sights, sounds, and smells of Pier 21 from dawn till dusk every day. It was a happy but often worrying experience, especially for those immigrants who did not have the right papers or passports. Immigration workers questioned these hopeful new Canadians. Doctors or nurses examined them.

If passengers failed to show the correct documents or were not in good health, there was a chance they might be sent back to their homeland. Those who passed inspection picked up their luggage, boarded trains, and travelled on to the towns that would be their new homes. They gazed out at the calm lakes and forests, and the wide-open skies of their new country.

The Home Children

Over one hundred thousand Home Children crossed the Atlantic to start new lives in Canada.

In the 1870s, there was not much chance that street kids in Britain would go to school. English John was one of many hundreds of poor children who lived on the streets, stealing food or money to stay alive. Many children had parents who could not afford to keep them and turned them out of their homes. Many died of hunger and sickness. British homes for **orphans** helped children who had lost their parents, had been turned out of their homes, or, like English John, had run away with nowhere to go.

"Home" children were kept in England for a time, then sent on ships to Canada or Australia. The girls worked in people's houses as servants, while the boys worked for farmers. The families who took them in promised to treat them like their own, but often boys and girls were treated badly. They were overworked and not given the pay that had been promised. Children ten years of age or older were made to do whatever work the host family wished.

Over the next sixty years, more than one hundred thousand children crossed the Atlantic Ocean to start a new life in Canada. After a while, most lost touch with their parents or could not remember them

"Barnardo Home" girls became domestic helpers in their new homes.

anymore because they were so young when they left home. English John was one of many who was sent to Canada, never to see his family again.

English John's Story (1898)

My father was a tin miner but he died when I was two. My mother married again and I didn't get along with my new father. He beat me, so I ran away from home when I was eight years old. The police found me and said I must live at my home or live at a Home for orphans. I made my choice. I would not go back home

These are some of the many Home Children put to work on Canadian farms who, like English John, carried water, fed the cows, and worked in the fields.

so they sent me to live for two years at the **Barnardo Home** in London, England.

There were so many children like me in the Home, with cruel parents they'd had to run away from. Some of them had no parents and had been taken from the streets of London. Some had parents who were too poor to feed them. The Barnardo Home was a good place because they gave us food and clothes. They called me a Home Child and promised me a better life.

One day, when I was ten, I learned that I would sail for Canada. I had never heard of it. They said I was to work on a farm near a city called Winnipeg. I got on a big ship called the *Labrador* with a group of my friends and we crossed the ocean. This was in 1898. We slept in bunks and the crossing was stormy so I was seasick for the whole voyage.

We docked at Pier 2 in Halifax, and they put me on a train with some of the children. We all had name tags hung around our necks as though we didn't know our own names! The whistle blew and we went for many days across the land of Canada. I saw cities and farms and wooden houses and fields. The farmer who took me in put me to work from sun-up to dark. I carried

Colonist trains carried immigrants from Pier 21 to their new homes in Canada. The trains were not comfortable for these long journeys. There was a coal-burning stove at each end of the car and only simple food items were sold. Passengers bought canned sardines, bread, butter, cheese, and fruits at the Pier 21 canteen to help them on their journey.

water and wood, fed the cows, washed the dishes, and I was only ten.

The farmer did not pay me or clothe me properly. The winter was cold and I could not keep warm. I had a pair of boots that did not fit and that let the snow in to chill my toes. I went to school for a little time but did not learn to read too well. I got tired of always working so hard with no pay, so I ran away, just as I did in England.

I went to many places, sleeping in barns, following the railroad tracks, and I sold the fish that I caught so I could buy bread. A **Saulteaux** family adopted me and I learned to trap for beaver and marten, fox and lynx. One time, we were in trouble when we were fishing in their canoe on the lake. A storm came up, our boat rocked, and my new family could not swim. We had

The unfamiliar sights and sounds of a new country were an exciting but exhausting experience for Home Children. This Home Child waits to meet his new family.

put our catch in a tub so I emptied the fish out of the tub, then I held up the tub for a sail. The tub caught the breeze and pushed us in to shore quickly.

The years went by. I learned the Cree and Saulteaux languages. I trapped for a living and I was happy to live in the flat prairies of Canada. It was

Home Children were sometimes treated unfairly, made to do the work expected of a man, and poorly fed and clothed.

better than the life I left in England. I married, and my wife knew how to shoot moose and deer, and how to skin them.

People called me English John because I lived like a Saulteaux but spoke English, and a reporter put my story in the local newspaper. What a day it was when that news travelled to England and my sister read it! She remembered me and knew I was the person in the newspaper story. She wrote to me and a friend helped me to answer her letters, but I never saw her again. She was too far away.

The Ukrainian Canadians

Michael was delighted to see dolphins swimming alongside their ship, the *Albertic*, as they sailed toward Halifax.

Michael was a Ukrainian boy who crossed the Atlantic with his mother, brothers, and sister. Michael's father had travelled ahead of them to work in Canada and saved enough to bring his family across the ocean. The Canadian government also lent money to immigrants like Michael's family to help them in their journey to Canada.

Michael's story (1929)

My dad was a gentle man, intelligent and brave. My family and I were all born in the Ukraine. Dad was a soldier for two years in the Austrian army and had to fight in some terrible wars. When he married and started his family, he wanted to give us all a better life than the one he knew, so he went to Canada ahead of us. He found a job cutting trees and clearing the land in Ontario, but then he was stranded in Canada when the First World War started.

> ### Pier 21 opens
>
> There were so many new Canadians entering that it was soon time to build a larger terminal in the south end of Halifax, one where ships could dock and embark their passengers, with the railway at its door. Pier 21 opened in 1928.

As soon as the war was over, he came back to our family in the Ukraine, and I was born in 1925. He stayed with us for another five years but his dream of giving us a better life in Canada never left him.

We were very poor, but we survived like everyone else, by growing vegetables and eating roots that grew wild. My father used to tell us that buying bread and butter cost a wheelbarrow of money in the Ukraine, but food was plentiful in Canada. When I was five, my dad left us again to follow his dream and find work in Canada. He boarded a rusting boat and earned his ticket by shovelling coal into the boilers. In 1929, he sent us money for our tickets.

I had two brothers and one sister, and we were all scared and excited at the same time to know that we were leaving our homeland. My mother did not speak English and she had only fifty dollars that my father had sent her, plus a few things from her old life. She knew she would never see her mother again but she was brave enough to leave and sail to Canada with the four of us.

We first sailed from Danzig[2] to Rotterdam and

Jobs for new Canadians

Michael and his family were among many who arrived at Pier 21 from the Ukraine. Some travelled on to Alberta or Saskatchewan to work on farms. Others, like Michael's father, found jobs as industrial workers in Montreal or southern Ontario. About seventy thousand Ukrainians arrived between 1924 and 1939.

2. The seaport of Danzig is now known as Gdańsk.

This Canada Post stamp commemorates the entry to Canada of Ukrainian immigrants.

then we took a ship, the *Albertic*, to Halifax. We arrived at Pier 21 in November 1929. I remember watching the prow of the ship break through the waves, and the dolphins that swam beside us. From Pier 21, my mother bought train tickets to Hamilton where my father had a job as a factory worker for the Westinghouse **foundry**. He picked us up at the train station in a brand new Essex car, and right away he tried to teach my mother to drive. She drove into the ditch on one side of the road, then drove across and landed in the ditch on the other side!

When the **Great Depression** started, my dad was out of work and had to sell the car, but he walked the eleven kilometres to Hamilton every day, looking for work. He would start at four o'clock in the morning for this long walk, and often when he arrived at the foundry gates,

> ## Mothers and children at Pier 21
>
> Women and children were given special care when they arrived at Pier 21. A nursery held twelve cribs and seven cots. There were baths and tubs for the mothers and babies, and Red Cross nurses were there to help. Every train had a woman conductor to help with children while they were on board.

The Ukrainian Canadians

FOTOGRAFJE — PHOTOGRAPHIES

Podpis
Signature

Katarzyna

Michael (lower right) and his family
pose for their passport photograph.

the guard would say, "Sorry, John, no work today." But
we survived.

We had a garden and the vegetables we grew were
kept in the root cellar and lasted through the winters.
We were poor as church mice but we were happy.
I'm thankful that my father was so brave, and willing
to follow his dream.

Without him, we could not have begun our lives in
Canada.

The Guest Children

British parents wanted their children to be safe, so they sent them on ships to Canada.

During the Second World War, Hitler's armies were bombing Britain from the sky. Parents wanted their children to be safe, so they sent them on ships

Who can come to Canada?

Eight thousand Guest Children crossed the ocean to Canada. The Canadian government said they wanted British boys and girls, but sadly, because of racial prejudice, they did not want Jewish children to come to Canada. Jewish children were called "refugees" and not "boys and girls."

They served their country

Five hundred throusand men and women left from Pier 21 to serve overseas. They are honoured on the Pier 21 museum's Wall of Service.

to Canada, Australia, New Zealand, or South Africa. Canada allowed British children, called Guest Children, to enter through Montreal and through Pier 21 in Halifax.

Jamie was a Scottish boy who came to Canada with other Guest Children from Scotland. Some Guest Children, like Jamie, waved goodbye with big smiles, excited about their new adventure. Others cried because they didn't want to go away from their mothers and fathers. Their parents said, "If things go wrong, remember you are British. Just grin and bear it."

Not all Guest Children arrived safely. Seventy-seven British children died

British parents said goodbye to their children, telling them, "If things go wrong, remember you are British. Just grin and bear it."

when a ship, the *City of Benares*, was sunk by a German submarine in September 1940. After this happened, no more children were sent across the ocean.

This is how one young English Guest girl, Patricia Balkar, remembers her arrival in Halifax in August 1940:

No one to wave goodbye

Canada entered the Second World War in 1939. Pier 21 was managed by the War Office and some five hundred thousand soldiers left from Pier 21 to cross the ocean and fight in Europe. These sailings were secret, and the troops left in darkness, with no one to watch or wave goodbye. Of these, fifty thousand died overseas, while thousands of wounded returned on hospital ships.

Coming into Halifax was like coming into fairyland. We sighted silver sands on the Nova Scotian coast and after three or four hours, we saw the harbour mouth, a beautiful place surrounded by forest-clad hills rather like a bristly doormat at the gates of a new land. The nicest part of all was to see the millions of unshielded harbour lights that night.[3]

Jamie's story (1940)

"Ciamar a tha sibh?" (How are you?) asked the customs officer in **Gaelic**.

These were the first words I heard when we docked at Pier 21. It was 1940, and Britain was at war. Scotland was my home, but my parents decided I must go to Canada for safety and stay with relatives until the war was over. Since I was only seven, Maggie, a friend of my

3. From "Across the Atlantic to Safety" by Michael Henderson, Halifax *Chronicle Herald*, September 5, 2010.

Meal times aboard the ship were a good opportunity to make new friends.

parents, came with me. She was going to be married to a Canadian so she would look after me on the ship, then take me on the train to London, Ontario.

"I hope I see a submarine," I told my father when we said goodbye. He was pleased that I wasn't afraid.

We had a good crossing and didn't see any other warships. We were on the *Duchess of York*, a very fast ship, and we made the crossing in nine days with eight hundred other Guest Children. I brought my

Guest Children arriving at Pier 21 after sunset were surprised to see the lights of Halifax. Their own countries were in darkness at night because of the war.

favourite book with me, *Babar the Elephant.* When we came into Pier 21 we met the customs officer who was from Cape Breton and knew Gaelic. Maggie didn't know any Gaelic and couldn't understand what he was saying to her. Well, he thought she was a spy, and he locked her in a detention area for the night. She was very upset. She thought she would never see me or her fiancé again. A Red Cross volunteer led me away to sleep in a dormitory in Pier 21.

It was all straightened out by the next morning

when Maggie was able to find her suitcase and show her papers. They freed her so that we could board the train to Kingston. I was wearing my Scottish kilt, so my relatives had no trouble finding me when we arrived.

A long separation

After leaving Britain, it would be as long as four years before children like Jamie saw their parents again. Mothers and fathers looked much older to them when they returned. Once they were back, the children had to go without the many kinds of food they had eaten in Canada.

The next four years were very happy ones, especially the summer vacations that I spent on a farm in the country. When I went back to Scotland four years later I took some food and also razor blades for my father, because there had been so much **rationing** in Britain during the war. I adjusted to life there, but I always wanted to return to Canada.

My four years in Canada as a child were very good ones and I never forgot the time I spent here. I married twenty years later and then brought my family back to Canada.

We've been happily settled here ever since.

The Jewish Orphans

Many Jewish children had spent most of their young lives hiding, living in ghettos, or sent to forced labour camps, or death camps. Hitler, the leader of the **Nazi** government in Germany, believed that Jews were a threat to Germany. He and his government punished the Jews, the Roma (sometimes called gypsies), the

Thousands of Jewish children went into hiding, sometimes surviving by sheer luck.

How it began

The Second World War began in 1939 when Germany, led by Hitler, attacked Poland. Britain and France declared war on Germany on September 3, 1939. Canada declared war on Germany one week later, on September 10, 1939. The war ended in 1945. Between 1947 and 1949, 1,123 homeless Jewish orphans came to Canada as part of the War Orphans Project.

disabled, and others who were "unwanted," and put them in work camps and death camps. From 1939 until 1943, Mariette and thousands like her went into hiding, sometimes surviving by sheer luck, but six million Jews were eventually captured and put to death.

A helping group, the Canadian Jewish Congress, offered to pay to bring these orphans from Europe to Canada, and found foster homes for them. When they arrived at Pier 21, these children knew it was the most important event in their lives. In time, they were able to feel a sense of freedom.

Jewish families in Canada also adopted Jewish orphans after the war. A special committee, the War Orphans Project, helped the children who had escaped Nazi **persecution**, making sure they were settled into their new lives. It found clothing, food, education, medical care, and homes for them in Canada.

Mariette's story (1947)

When we children walked down the gangplank, there was barbed wire on both sides of us and bars on the windows of the building. The officials asked our names but gave us numbers to wear on cardboard tags. I had lost my identity yet again.

The officials searched our belongings. When they gave back our things, the diamond was missing from a ring that my sister had given me, and my money had been taken. We were too afraid to say anything. They questioned us and made us feel like criminals. There were no smiles. This was Pier 21 in 1947.

I lost my mother, my brothers, my grandparents, and my aunts and uncles in the death camps and

These Jewish Orphans wait with their guardian to meet their foster parents.

I had spent my life so far running and hiding from the Nazis. Canadian Jewish Congress had brought us to Canada.

From Pier 21, we took the train to Montreal and though I spoke French and seven other languages,

Congress Bulletin

VOLUME 4, NUMBER 9. — MONTREAL, CANADA — SEPTEMBER 1947

Failure Faces Orphans Movement
Unless Homes are Found for Them

JIAS ASSISTS EVERY PHASE OF PROJECT

Joseph Kage, assistant to the National Executive Director of the Jewish Immigrant Aid Society of Canada, has been loaned by his organization to the orphaned youth movement which the Canadian Jewish Congress

Joseph Kage

is sponsoring from Europe. Mr. Kage, who as an experienced social worker has been on the staff of McGill University before coming to the JIAS, has been placed in charge of the reception center in Montreal, and supervises the group activities and the adjustment process of these youngsters before they are placed in foster homes. At the same time each of these young immigrants is attached to a trained social worker who assists in his personal problems together with the Big Brother or the Big Sister who will volunteer for this work.

Mr. Kage has also been associated with the Family Welfare Bureau of the Federation
(Continued on page 5)

The youngest member of the European refugee children to land on these shores is seen disembarking from a specially-chartered plane which brought them from Halifax to Montreal. Some older members of the party are following her.

Two Groups In Canada; Third Is Now En Route

The second group of war orphans arrived in the Dominion during the second Succoth week-end. They stayed over in Halifax for two days to avoid travelling on the festival and homes were arranged in the community for them by the local Congress committee and by the sisterhood of the Roble Street Synagogue. Noah Heinish, honorary vice-president of the Congress is supervising the arrangements. The sisterhood committee consists of Mesdames A. Newman, Charles Aron, R. Guldfarb, Julie Silverman and Nathan Rubin.
(Continued on page 2)

JEWISH FOSTER HOMES URGENTLY NEEDED FOR ALL

The most serious difficulty facing the arrangements committee in charge of the movement of war orphans from Europe to this country is the shortage of foster homes in which these young people can be placed. Spokesmen of the committee are frank in stating that unless many more homes are immediately found for this project the entire movement may be jeopardized.

David Weiss, director of the Family and Child Welfare Bureau of the Federation of Jewish Philanthropies of Montreal, outlined for the Congress Bulletin the nature of the needs.

"The children coming are all in their teens; they are healthy, cheerful, well-bred youngsters, considerate and alert, and the social workers of the Jewish Child Welfare Bureau who are assisting in the project speak highly of the contribution that these youngsters can make to home life.

"We are looking for Jewish homes where these young people can find a place to sleep and to eat, perhaps where they can bring their friends or where they can find boys and girls for whom they would be
(Continued on page 2)

Montreal Readers Please See Page 16

After the war, Canada slowly began to open its doors to young orphans like Mariette.

I didn't understand the French spoken there. After twenty minutes of listening to the Montreal French, I told my guardian I could not live there.

The next town was Winnipeg. I lived there for three weeks, but I hated the snow and cold. I asked to live somewhere else. Calgary was next.

I looked outside and I said, "Where is this place?" It was just little red buildings by the train station. "I can't stay here, I have to go into a city so I can get lost."

I was a hidden child all my life, never speaking, pretending to be deaf and dumb, trying to camouflage myself.

Vancouver was next. There were one thousand Jewish families living here and it was an easier place to hide. I wanted to be beside the ocean. In fact, my earliest memories were spending happy days at the beach with my family in Brussels.

I met my foster family in Vancouver, but ran away from them twelve times in the first year. My foster

Remembering MS *St. Louis*

The Wheel of Conscience, a monument at Pier 21, is a memorial to the 932 Jewish refugees aboard the MS *St. Louis* who were turned away from Canada on the eve of the Second World War. The ship was refused entry to many ports in Europe, then it crossed the ocean seeking refuge, but the Canadian government refused to offer safe harbour, even though the ship sailed very close to Halifax. After being turned away by the United States, the ship eventually returned to Europe, where 254 of its passengers died during the Holocaust.

The doors slowly open

At the end of the Second World War there were 250,000 refugees who had no homes. During the war, the Canadian Jewish community asked the Canadian government to accept Jewish refugees, but Canada and other countries refused to take them. After the war, Pier 21 was an arrivals gate when Canada slowly began to open its doors to young orphans like Mariette. By the year 2000, Canada had become one of the largest refugee receiving countries in the world.

father would bring me back and say, "No matter how far you go, you belong to us. This is your family now."

I owe much to him, his wife, and to my first teacher in Canada. She understood how much I needed to learn. I had missed school for many years and she helped me complete fourteen years of school in only seven and a half years. I read books, as many as I could find.

I am always hungry to read and learn more. We survivors are always hungry for knowledge. Now I have been president and fundraiser of many organizations, and a public speaker for the Holocaust Education Centre. It is my way of paying back my community and my country.

The Estonian Canadians

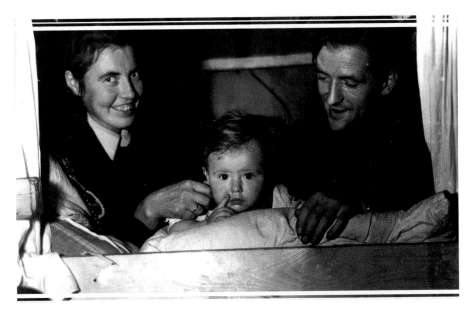

This little family smiles a greeting from their small sleeping quarters aboard the *Walnut*.

Heili, a young Estonian girl, had to leave her homeland. Estonia was ruled by Russia from 1910 till 1991 and Heili's family, along with other Estonians, did not want to live under Russian Communist rule. Many Estonians escaped to Sweden but were forced to return to Estonia and then punished in Siberian work camps. Others were determined never to go

With only the clothes on their backs

Besides the Estonians, there were many in Europe without homes or money at the end of the Second World War. Refugees like Heili were forced to leave their country because their lives and homes had been destroyed by war. One hundred thousand refugees came into Canada through Pier 21 following the war. They came with only the clothes they were wearing. They had no money and no papers, and no one to take them in.

In time, Canadians understood the needs of these people and they were met with a kind welcome at Pier 21. The Girl Guides, Boy Scouts, church groups, YWCA, Red Cross—all were responsible for meeting the refugees.

back to their home country, so they bought a boat called the *Walnut* that would bring them across the rough north seas to Canada.

The *Walnut* had room for only 18, but there were 347 people who wanted to sail to freedom. They were determined to go, no matter the conditions on the ship, so they stacked the bunk beds like cells in a bee's honeycomb. They set out from Sweden on November 13, 1948. The voyage lasted a month and it was a stormy crossing to Sydney, Nova Scotia, and at last on to Pier 21 in Halifax. They had made the journey with

These children were on the *Walnut* together with Heili for the long Atlantic crossing.

very little food and without heat or radio equipment. Heili's father was captain of this ship.

Heili's Story (1948)

I was walking on the beach with my dog and I knew that soon I would never see my pet again. My family and I had to leave our home in Estonia and run away to Sweden or we might be sent to prison camps. I was only eleven when we began our escape. When we were safely inside Sweden, we had to run away again, to Canada this time. My little sister and I picked two sets of clothes, one set to wear, and one to take in my parents' suitcases. I brought two of my favourite books. One was about a boy and a beaver, and the other was called *Pippi Longstocking*.

We boarded a small but strong ship with hundreds of other people. It was called the *Walnut*. Everyone on board had given money to buy the ship. My dad was the captain, so my family stayed in a cabin on deck. The others were not so lucky. They slept in the hold underneath and they were very seasick, especially when there were storms. They could not eat, but I was only seasick one time and then I was fine.

The voyage to Halifax took almost one month. It was a very stormy crossing.

It took us three weeks to cross the stormy ocean to Canada, but at last we were there. I hoped I would find a beaver for a pet, just like the boy in my book. The sky and the sea were grey and it was wintertime when we landed in Halifax and walked up the gangway into Pier 21.

There were boxes of warm clothes inside, and we picked out things to wear. We ate in the big dining hall where an artist on our boat hung all the drawings he had done of us during the voyage. I wanted to be an artist like him when I saw those pictures. I had Coca-Cola and bubblegum for the first time in my life. I had never tasted such a sweet drink.

I couldn't sleep that first night, since I was so used to the rocking motion of the ship and the sound of the waves and now everything was still. We stayed for a few weeks in Pier 21 and everyone was very kind to us. We even had a big Christmas tree and presents.

Soon it was time to take the train to Vancouver and we crossed the country, over the flat prairies and through the Rocky Mountains with their huge canyons. We rented a cabin for the first winter, and my sister and I started school. I only knew a little English, and could say, "What is your name?" and "Here is my pencil," but I learned very quickly. Every day after school, I looked in the woods near our cabin for beavers, but I couldn't find any. I still wanted one for a pet.

I am an artist now and, of course, I am all grown up. I live in a beautiful place, here in British Columbia. From my window, I can see mountains and ocean, but in my heart I am always looking for shelters. I express this in my art. I like to build sculptures that people can walk inside.

Canada has been my shelter. Canada was my destiny and I knew right away that this was where I belonged. My life would be so different if we had not come to Canada.

Cornflakes and tobacco

Companies began to give gifts to the immigrants. They hoped that new Canadians would remember these gifts and buy more of their products. Some gave tobacco and cigarettes. The Kellog company gave small boxes of cornflakes, but many immigrants had only ever used corn to feed cattle. Soon the floor of Pier 21 was covered with cornflakes from opened and discarded boxes.

The War Brides

When the ship docked at Pier 21, bands, waving flags, and cheering crowds welcomed the war brides and their children.

After the Second World War was over, 48,000 brides, along with their 22,000 children, were still anxiously waiting to join their husbands in Canada. Susie, the daughter of a war bride, crossed the ocean on the luxury liner *Queen Mary* with her mother and brothers, along with other war brides. The liner had been used as a troop ship during the war, and then refitted again to carry war brides and their children. When the ship docked at Pier 21, the war brides saw bands playing, flags waving, and cheering crowds. An honour guard of Mounties waited at the pier, and the Red Cross and Salvation Army served tea and refreshments to the weary but happy brides and their children.

Susie's story (1948)

Roast duck, ice cream, tables filled with so much food, and everything so delicious! We had never seen bread so white. It was 1948 and I was ten years old. I had lived through the war with my family in England where food was rationed. Now, here we were in a ship's dining room and there was food of every kind. We couldn't believe it. No wonder so many passengers were sick—no one was used to eating like this.

My mother was a war bride. My two brothers and I were on the *Queen Mary* with her, crossing the ocean to be with our new dad. My real father had died when

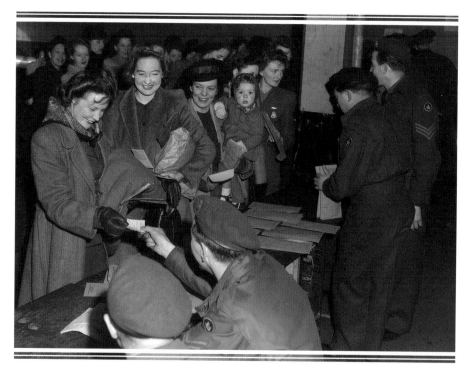

British customs officials check immigration papers before the war brides board their ship to Canada.

I was very young and now we were starting life with our new father. He was a Canadian soldier my mother had met when he was in England.

I missed my friends very much, but there was so much to do and see on our ship. There were hundreds of war brides sailing with us, and many had babies with them. My mother was a little older than the other brides, and they came to her for advice about caring for their babies during the voyage. I saw movies and wandered the ship with my two older brothers.

The crossing took four days. When we arrived at Pier 21, a band played at the dock to welcome us, and people gave us chocolates and candy. Our new dad was there to meet us, but first we went into the immigration hall, where we saw alphabet letters on cards posted on the walls. We stood under the letter for our family name, and Red Cross volunteers helped us find our luggage and our train.

We took the train with the other war brides. Many of them were going west and the train made stops along the way. At each station stop, we would look out the windows and watch war brides getting off to be met by their husbands. There was always a

New brides...

War brides, like Susie's mother, were those women who married Canadian servicemen in Britain and the rest of Europe. Canadians were among the first to help Britain after war was declared in 1939 and they spent more time there than any other member of the Allied Forces.

...and new children

Even though bombs were falling and danger was everywhere, some 48,000 young women married or became engaged to Canadian servicemen during the Second World War. Like Susie's mother, these war brides were mostly from Britain, but a few thousand were also from other places: the Netherlands, Belgium, France, Italy, and Germany. After the war, until 1948, twenty-two thousand children crossed the Atlantic with their mothers.

band playing to welcome them. Often, strangers boarded the train just to say hello and give us little welcome gifts. It was such a happy and exciting trip for everyone!

Our first year in Canada was a year to remember: the first day at our new school, the first heavy snowfall, our first long, hot summer— such a jumble of memories! One time I went to supper at a friend's house and she led me to the cellar to show me shelves full of preserved fruit. I was allowed to choose whatever fruit I wanted for dessert. I had never seen so much food in one pantry. In England, all our food had been rationed, and I had been lucky to see an orange once a year at Christmas.

The dining room was Susie's favourite place on the *Queen Mary*. Because of the wartime rationing, she had never seen so much delicious food.

At each stop on their long journey, passengers would look out the windows and watch the war brides getting off the train to meet their husbands.

I often think about those times and our voyage on that beautiful ship. I saw the movie *Titanic* twice, just to see the *Queen Mary* again. I visited Pier 21 when it first opened as a museum, and felt happy to be back. There is something about Pier 21, as though it is alive with memories that everyone shared, coming to Canada and starting new lives. It is such a special place.

The Dutch Canadians

Two little girls wear their traditional Dutch clothing. Note the Dutch wooden shoes.

Many Dutch people moved to Canada after the war, including Dutch war brides. There is a close friendship between Canada and the Netherlands because Canadian soldiers helped to free the Netherlands from German rule during the Second World War. During the war, Canada was home to

An immigration officer examines the travel documents of a Dutch family who are on their way to Canada.

Princess Juliana and other members of the Dutch royal family. Each May, the Canadian Tulip Festival in Ottawa helps to remember the Princess with a beautiful display of Dutch tulips, sent from the Netherlands.

Maryke and her family were among the many Dutch immigrants who chose to live in Canada after the war.

Maryke's Story (1950)

I sat on a bench with my two little brothers at Pier 21. We were wearing our Dutch wooden shoes. A Canadian man thought we were quite cute with our blond, curly hair and blue eyes, so he bought us each a chocolate bar. That was my first taste of Canada.

I was born and raised in Holland. During the Second World War, the German **occupation** in Holland made our lives hard but we were luckier than some. Although food was rationed, my father had worked for a farmer and could get milk and vegetables for us, and sometimes meat.

Maryke's mother felt that Canada would be a safer place for her family, free from wars.

What's in the box?

Dutch immigrants usually brought their belongings in large wooden crates. At Pier 21, customs officers would joke that they brought everything but the kitchen sink. One morning, they opened one of the boxes and found a kitchen sink inside!

Maryke, with her father and her two brothers, pose beside the large trunk that held their belongings.

We left Holland just after the war was over and came to Canada because we knew there was good land here for farming, much more than in Holland. My father had five brothers who wanted to farm, and it was impossible to find land for all of them in Holland. He wanted to work his own farm. My mother felt Canada would be a safer place, free from wars.

My parents wanted the best for us, so as soon as the war was over, we boarded a ship to Canada. We could take only a little money with us, but we were allowed one trunk that was big enough to put some possessions in, things that were useful, like bedding, books, cooking utensils, small furniture. We would not see that trunk again until a month after we arrived in Canada. The voyage took eleven days. It was often stormy and many people were seasick.

Maryke's two brothers enjoy their first Canadian winter.

We arrived at Pier 21, then took a train to a little farming community in Ontario and began our new lives. My mother was homesick, so what a feast it was for her when the trunk arrived in Canada a month later with all its reminders of our home inside.

I learned my first word in English when I played with the neighbour child. She asked me if I wanted some candy, and when I didn't understand, she went inside her house to bring me some. "Candy" was the first word that I learned in Canada.

After a year of school, I could read books very well. My favourite was *Heidi*, and I loved the story of *Black Beauty*.

Dutch immigrants wait in the immigration hall of Pier 21 to have their papers checked.

My parents were lonely at first, and I remember on summer evenings we would often all walk the two kilometres to the nearest farm to visit. Sometimes we would stay for supper.

We are forever grateful to the Canadian people who welcomed us and helped us during our first years in Canada.

The Hungarian Canadians

These Hungarians wait anxiously in Vienna, Austria, for the train that will take them to their ship.

In 1956, the people of Hungary rose up against Communist rule and because of this, Soviet Russian troops punished the people with tanks and bombs. Life in Hungary was impossible for its people. Three weeks after the Russian troops invaded, Eva and her mother were among 200,000 refugees who escaped

Volunteer groups such as the Red Cross, or Sisters of Service, were very important in helping immigrants to be comfortable when they disembarked at Pier 21.

to Austria. Canada welcomed 37,500 Hungarian refugees, and these people were quickly helped to find jobs and homes here.

Eva's Story (1956)

"Don't worry, those bullets are not coming toward us. They're going away from us," said my neighbours.

I knew they were lying to try and make me feel safer. My girlfriend and I had been visiting, minutes before the Russian soldiers suddenly began to attack with their tanks and bombs, and take over my city, Budapest. We had to stay with my neighbours for the night and the next morning when we came out, our city was in ruins.

You see, there was a revolution happening in my country because we all wanted to be free of **Communism**. We wanted to be free to choose our own leaders.

When I arrived home at last, my mother had been so afraid for my safety. She knew we had to leave and go

Freedom of information

Radio Free Europe is an American radio broadcast that is transmitted to people in countries that do not have freedom of information. The broadcasts present news and information or a different point of view to countries in the Middle East, Central Asia, and Eastern Europe.

Governments in these countries often make it illegal for their citizens to listen to Radio Free Europe broadcasts because they do not want their people to know what is happening in the world. They stop the transmissions by jamming the programs. Jamming is done by sending radio signals that create a loud noise to prevent listeners from hearing a broadcast.

> **So many fir trees!**
>
> One new Canadian who arrived at Christmastime was amazed to see so many fir trees being sold in Halifax. He cut down a fir tree, not knowing it was a protected tree inside Point Pleasant Park. He brought it back to Pier 21, and the immigration officers there kept quiet about it and allowed him to decorate it for Christmas.

to my older brother in Spain, but when she asked him, he told her it was better for us to go to Canada. Every night we listened to Radio Free Europe to hear the truth about what was happening in our country. It was against the law to listen to this program, and we had to keep the sound down very low, especially when the broadcast made a shrill noise that might alert unfriendly neighbours who would then report us.

Many of our friends came to us every night and clustered around the radio, listening for some hopeful news that might tell us we were finally free from Communism. Always, someone's hand was on the knob to turn the sound down, just in case that shrill jamming sound suddenly came to drown out the broadcast.

We were hungry much of the time. Our food was

These Hungarian family members, representing three generations, are proud to receive their Canadian citizenship papers together.

cut off. We kept our clothes packed near our beds in case we had to leave suddenly in the night. One night, it was time to go. My mother and I took our two satchels of things that were most precious to us, and we walked toward Austria with other refugees.

We travelled many hours in the darkness, then stopped to rest in a safe farmhouse and settled

Translators at Pier 21 were on hand to help these new Canadians.

down to sleep. A border guard threw open the door. "You are under arrest!" he shouted. He told us that we would be shot for running away from Hungary. We gave him all our family money and jewels so that he would not report us. He turned his back on us and told us to go.

We walked quickly away toward the border, sure

that at any moment we would be stopped. We trudged through the muddy fields till the leather soles of my shoes began to come apart. We came to a village that sparkled with pretty blue lights.

We were in Austria, at last!

We spent a few days in a camp there waiting to board a ship that would leave from Vienna. On the day we were to leave, my mother went into a deli and bought me an orange and a banana. I had never tasted a banana in my life but had always wanted to try one. It turned out I hated the taste of it and cannot eat bananas to this day. How funny that I had wanted to try one since I was very little only to find I didn't like them.

We sailed on the *Saxonia* on January 25, 1957, with two hundred Hungarians and about three hundred other immigrants. My mother had a document for me that said "plus one child." She told me if I didn't behave, she would find another child as her "plus one."

Pier 21 was filled with hundreds of people when we arrived in Halifax. We were herded into the immigration hall, and some children thought we

At Pier 21, workers divided the Hungarian refugees into two groups with women and girls in one, men and boys in the other. Then they boarded buses to spend their first night at a hospital in Halifax that had been converted to two separate sleeping quarters for them. A young boy kept trying to enter the women's area. Finally, "he" explained that she was a girl who had only been able to escape from her homeland dressed as a boy. Because she had short hair, she had been classified as a boy when she arrived at Pier 21.

were going into a giant fish, because *hal* means "fish" in Hungarian. I knew it meant a large room because I knew some English already. There was a counter at Pier 21 that had donations of clothes and shoes. I quickly found some shoes to replace my worn out, falling apart shoes, and put them on my feet right away. I found some clothes that fit me. Our train was waiting so we were rushed through.

We started our new life in Winnipeg and lived in an apartment close to the Hudson's Bay Company. I would go there at lunchtime with my girlfriends to look at, touch, and sniff the bottles at the cosmetics counter. To this day, I thank the salespeople at the Bay. When we saw all the cosmetics and perfumes with their fragrances, we opened up the containers, as many as we could, and sniffed them, over and over. The salespeople let us. Somehow, they knew my friends and I needed to do this to enjoy new experiences, and to express our new sense of personal freedom. We never knew this freedom during our lives in Hungary.

My grandchildren today are so used to having hundreds of different choices for everything they buy. When we came to Canada we had so many choices, so much freedom. Whenever we met with our friends for a meal we would put a big bowl of whipped cream on the table to go with dessert. We were saying, "You see? We made the right choice to come here. Look at me! I can put all this whipped cream on the table!"

The Italian Canadians

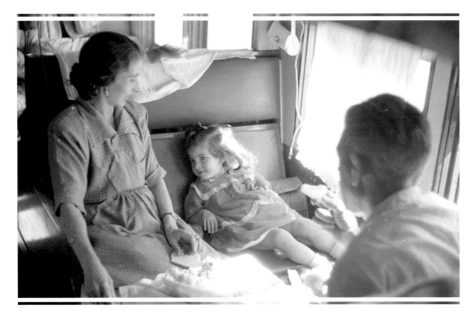

When Luigi's mother saw the snow-covered fields from the train window, she said, "Where have we come to? Siberia?"

Luigi and his family were among thousands of Italian immigrants who arrived in Canada after 1948. When the war ended, there were many more jobs to be found in Canada than in Italy. Italians wanted a better life and they knew this was their chance to find it. Italians were often greeted at Pier 21 by the Italian

Vice-Consul to Canada. In one year alone, thirty thousand Italian immigrants came through Pier 21.

Luigi's story (1961)

"Where did all these beans come from?" people were asking.

There were little white beans all over the floor in the customs room at Pier 21. My mother had packed beans into her trunk but one corner was damaged and they had spilled.

"Don't tell them they're ours," whispered my mother, "or we'll get in trouble."

We had just finished our long voyage from Naples, Italy, on the *Saturnia.* My sister and mother had been seasick for the whole voyage, but I explored the ship with another boy from my hometown while they stayed below.

When we finally arrived at Pier 21 there were lots of suitcases and trunks in the warehouse. We had to find our luggage, then have it checked by a customs officer who would confiscate items that were not allowed into Canada. We saw a long table

Shelter, food, and kindness

Skilled workers were needed in cities and on farms. If there were no jobs, they lived at Pier 21 while they looked for full-time work. They would help to clear snow off the railway lines outside Pier 21, and go into Halifax to look for jobs. One new Canadian wrote, "We were happy, we had shelter, food, and kind and friendly immigration officers. We felt protected, sheltered, not jailed."

loaded with prosciutto, liquor, sausages, cheese, and salamis. People thought they might starve before they got started in Canada so they had packed these items in their luggage.

One man was so proud of a prosciutto he had made and brought from Italy. He said he couldn't wait to share it with his relatives when he arrived in Toronto. Well, it was confiscated by customs and put on this table with all the other food that was not allowed to be brought into Canada.

We could not speak English, but the customs officers were very kind to us and made sure we found the right train. My mother had brought an Italian-English dictionary from Italy, but accidentally left it on the ship and didn't know how to ask for it back.

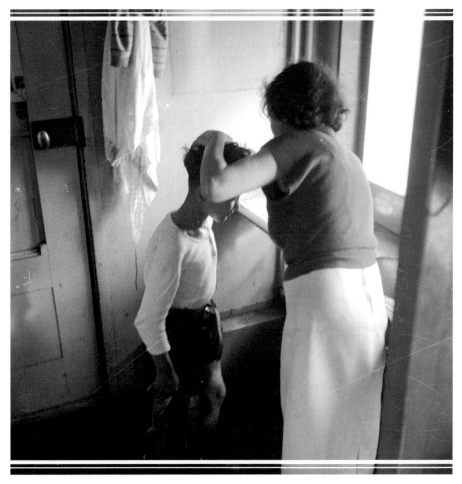

An Italian boy and his sister tidy themselves up before their train arrives in Toronto. Luigi had not seen his father for many years and did not recognize him when they met at the train station.

We tried to eat the bread and spaghetti they served on the train, but it was too sweet and we refused to eat it. It was November, and the train passed by snow-covered fields and villages. "Where have we come to? Siberia?" my mother asked.

My father met us at the station in Toronto where he was working in construction. He left for Canada when I was three. Now I was seven and I didn't remember him, but my older sister Maria ran to him and hugged him.

I went to school and adjusted quickly to the new language and to my new life. I had a good teacher, Mrs. Iablonski, who gave me extra help in English, because her parents had come from Poland and she knew what it was like being in a new country.

There were no **ESL** classes for new Canadians the way there are today. The first books I read in English were *Curious George* and *Babar the Elephant.* My sister's teacher was not so helpful and she had a tougher time learning to speak English.

Luigi's mother could not speak English, but a customs officer helped them find the right train.

The other kids called us names at first and storekeepers were impatient that we didn't yet know how to ask for our groceries, but gradually we all adjusted. We got used to Canada and decided we were not going back to Italy. Jobs were scarce in Italy, we were a farming family, and education was expensive there. Canada was our home now.

I visited Pier 21 again, later in my life. I'm pleased it has become a national museum. It's a wonderful way to remember all those who made the journey to Canada.

The Last Years at Pier 21

The Czechoslovakian Canadians

In 1968, Czechoslovakian refugees arrived, and some stayed at Pier 21 until they found homes in Halifax. They had left their home country during the Prague Spring Uprising, when Russian tanks had invaded their country.

Salt cod and ice cream!

Cuban immigrants arrived at Pier 21 by way of Gander, Newfoundland. About one hundred stayed at the sleeping quarters in Pier 21 while they waited for visas that would bring them to the United States. They enjoyed salt cod, and were happy to find so much of it in Halifax. They would soak it in hot water, then cover it with chopped onions, hard-boiled egg, and sauce. One of the customs officers entered a random-dial radio contest and won twenty-five dollars. He used the money to buy large amounts of cake and ice cream for the children.

In 2011, Pier 21 became the "Canadian Museum of Immigration at Pier 21," which honours each new Canadian, as they have helped to make Canada the great country that it is today.

A new age

By 1971, the age of passenger planes had begun and Pier 21 was no longer needed to welcome new Canadians. Planes were a better way to travel than the great ocean liners. Now there were regular flights across the Atlantic, and it was cheaper and easier to travel this way. Pier 21 had served for almost fifty years, sending over one million hopeful refugees and immigrants on to their new lives, taking care of their needs and offering them an example of the refuge they would find in Canada.

In 2011, Pier 21 changed its official name to the Canadian Museum of Immigration at Pier 21. It is now Canada's sixth national museum. The museum's new goal is to tell the stories of all

Canada Post paid tribute to new Canadians with commemorative stamps like this one.

the people from all parts of the world who came to Canada from 1867 to the present, and through each of the gateways from east to west. Pier 21 recognizes that it is important to honour people of all races and creeds. Each played a key role in helping to shape Canada and make it the great country that it is today, a nation of people from different places, living side by side like the patterns in a lovely, colourful quilt. Voted by Canadians as one of the seven wonders of

Canada, Pier 21 continues to tell thousands of stories, like those of Mariette, Eva, English John, Luigi, and the many others who came to Canada. At the museum, you can pull up a chair and listen to their taped voices or read their handwritten journals. Pier 21 has kept the stories and photographs of those who arrived or departed: the refugees, the troops, the war brides, the wartime evacuees, and other new Canadians, and it has added new stories. From the large windows, visitors to Pier 21 can see the mouth of Halifax Harbour, where the very first hopeful immigrants arrived to begin their lives on these shores.

The Maple Leaf forever!

In 1965, the Union Jack, the old flag of Canada, was lowered, and the new Maple Leaf flag raised. The immigrants at Pier 21 came out to observe the ceremony, and cheered and applauded as the new Canadian flag was raised.

Timeline

1749:　　the City of Halifax is founded.

1869:　　British Child Emigration Movement begins and Home Children arrive at Pier 2.

1898:　　English John arrives in Canada.

1917:　　Pier 2 destroyed in the Halifax Explosion.

1928:　　Pier 21 opens.

1929:　　Beginning of Great Depression; Michael arrives in Canada from the Ukraine.

1939–40:　Canada enters the Second World War; troops embark from Pier 21.

1940:　　Beginning of Guest Children arrivals at Pier 21, including Jamie.

1942–48:　48,000 war brides and 22,000 children land at Pier 21.

1944:　　A serious fire at Pier 21 leads to some rebuilding.

1947:　　Mariette arrives in Canada with other Jewish orphans; beginning of Dutch immigration.

1947–48:　Baltic refugees flee their country.

1948:	Heili arrives in Canada with her mother. Susie and her mother arrive in Canada on the *Queen Mary* with other war brides.
1949:	Fifty thousandth refugee arrives at Pier 21.
1950:	Maryke and her family arrive in Canada from the Netherlands; German immigration begins.
1956:	Hungarian uprising; 37,500 Hungarian refugees are admitted to Canada, including Eva and her family.
1961–63:	Cubans are housed at Pier 21 on their way to the US.
1961:	Luigi and his family arrive in Canada from Italy.
1965:	Immigrants at Pier 21 cheer the raising of the Maple Leaf flag.
1971:	Immigration Services leave Pier 21.
1988:	Pier 21 Society is formed.
2011:	Pier 21 becomes the National Museum of Immigration.

Recommended Reading

Charlie: A Home Child's Life in Canada by Beryl Young

Orphan at My Door: the home child diary of Victoria Cope by Jean Little

Home Child by Barbara Haworth Attard

The Sky is Falling, Looking at the Moon, and *The Lights Go On Again* by Kit Pearson

The Diary of a Young Girl by Anne Frank

Hannah's Suitcase by Karen Levine

Turned Away by Carol Matas

The Language of Doves by Rosemary Wells

Number the Stars by Lois Lowry

In Flanders Fields: The story of the Poem by John McCrae by Linda Granfield

High Flight: A story of World War II by Linda Granfield

A Bloom of Friendship: The Story of the Canadian Tulip Festival by Anne Renaud

Refugee Child: My Memories of the 1956 Hungarian Revolution by Bobby Kalman

The Wall: Growing up Behind the Iron Curtain by Peter Sis

The Sandwich by Ian Wallace

Pier 21: Stories from Near and Far by Anne Renaud

Pier 21: The Gateway That Changed Canada by Trudy Duivenvoorden Mitic and J. P. Leblanc

The Kids Book of Canadian Immigration by Deborah Hodge and John Mantha

Acknowledgements

The author is grateful to all those who gave their time, stories, and assistance to this project.

Thanks go to Nabiha Atallah; Sydney Baker; Grace Bell, Chronicle Herald Library Archives; Marion Crawford; Maryke DeJong; Marie Doduck; W. J. Douglas; Max Eisen; Celie Halzel; Emma Jolly; Eva Kende; Anna Kertz; Heili Linde; Susan Marcus, Canadian Jewish Congress; Evelyn Merriam; Frieda Miller, Vancouver Holocaust Education Centre; Luigi Pagano; Susie Pitul; Melba Roellinghoff; Janice Rosen, Archives, Canadian Jewish Congress Charities Committee; Ellen Scheinberg, Ontario Jewish Archives; Elizabeth Shaffer, Vancouver Holocaust Education Centre Archives; Pieta Settimi and the family of the late Michael Schwedyk; and to my editor, Whitney Moran.

Image Credits

Author's Collection: 15, 20, 51, 52, 53
Canadian Jewish Congress Committee National Archives: 32
Heili Linde: 37
Library and Archives Canada: 2, 5, 7, 9, 10, 13, 14, 18, 21, 39, 44, 47, 48, 49, 50, 54, 55, 59, 60, 64, 67, 69, 72
Manivald Sein: 39
Max Kalm: 35
Nova Scotia Archives: cover (main image), 23, 25, 26, 42, 56
United States Holocaust Memorial Museum: 28, 31
Whitney Moran: 71

Glossary

Allied Forces: at the start of World War Two, France, Poland, and the United Kingdom were allied against Germany. Other countries soon joined them.

Barnardo Homes: homes for orphans in Britain, founded by Dr. Thomas J. Barnardo.

Communism: a way of government led by one political party in which all goods are shared equally, and citizens lose the right to hold private property as well as the right to express their religious beliefs.

Colonist: a person who settles in a new country.

Confiscate: to take away or seize private property, by authority or law.

ESL: English as a Second Language; an English class offered in schools to help new Canadians to learn English as their second language.

Foundry: a factory where liquid metal is poured into shapes or moulds, then cooled to create machinery parts. Today, the work is usually done by machines.

Gaelic: a language that is spoken in Scotland and Ireland.

Great Depression: period from 1929–1939, when there were no jobs to be found and many businesses failed.

Holocaust: the killing of an estimated six million Jews and other people by the Nazis during the Second World War.

Immigrant: a person who travels to a country and settles there; its root word is "migrate."

Immigration: the act of coming into a country to settle there.

Nazi: a member of the National Socialist German Workers' Party, founded in Germany, 1919, and brought to power by Adolf Hitler in 1933.

Occupation:	many countries in Europe were taken over by the armies of Nazi Germany in World War Two.
Orphan:	a child who has lost one or usually both parents.
Persecute:	to cause suffering especially among those of different racial or religious groups.
Pier:	a platform stretching into the water used as a landing place for ships and boats.
Prosciutto:	(proh-shoo-toh) a kind of Italian ham.
Rations:	a fixed amount of food or products given to people when there is not enough for everyone.
Refugee:	a person who has run away from danger or problems in his or her home country.
Saulteaux:	(soh-toh) a member of a First Nations people living in Ontario, Manitoba, and Saskatchewan; a division of the Ojibwa tribe.

Index

Index